Tow Trucks

BY CYNTHIA AMOROSO

The Child's World

Published by The Child's World®
1980 Lookout Drive • Mankato, MN 56003-1705
800-599-READ • www.childsworld.com

Acknowledgments
The Child's World®: Mary Berendes, Publishing Director
The Design Lab: Design
Jody Jensen Shaffer; Editing
Pamela J. Mitsakos: Photo Research

Photos
Blade_kostas/iStock.com: 16; danishkhan/iStock.
com: 15; David M. Budd Photography: 8, 11; David
Touchtone/123RF.com: cover, 1; Evok20/Shutterstock.
com: 7; Mike Clarke /iStock.com: 4,19, 20; Slobo
Mitic/iStock.com: 12

ISBN 9781623239701
LCCN 2013947256

Printed in the United States of America
Mankato, MN
November, 2013
PA02190

Contents

This tow truck is taking a car to a repair shop.

4

What are tow trucks?

Tow trucks are special kinds of **vehicles**. They pull or carry other vehicles. They are specially made for this job.

How are tow trucks used?

Tow trucks pull vehicles that cannot move on their own. Sometimes cars and trucks get in crashes. Sometimes they break down and will not run. Tow trucks take cars and trucks to places where people can fix them.

LODGING – EXIT 201

This tow truck is pulling a car from a snowbank.

cab

engine

8

What are the parts of a tow truck?

In the front, a tow truck looks like other trucks. It has a **cab** for the driver. The back of the truck looks different. It has special parts for towing other vehicles. These parts get their power from the truck's **engine**. The engine's power moves the truck, too.

Many tow trucks have a large arm on the back. The arm is called a **boom**. The end of the boom sometimes has a hook. The hook is on a long cable. A **winch** winds the cable and raises the hook.

winch

boom

You can see the tow bar underneath this car.

How do tow trucks tow?

Many tow trucks use a tow bar. The tow bar goes under one end of the vehicle. The tow truck raises the tow bar. Only two of the vehicle's wheels stay on the ground. The tow truck pulls the vehicle easily.

Many tow trucks use wheel lifts. The lifts go under the front or back wheels. The tow truck raises the wheel lifts. Then it pulls the vehicle along.

You can see how
the wheel lift is only
raising the front wheels
of this damaged car.

This flatbed tow truck is carrying a damaged car.

Some tow trucks carry vehicles instead of towing them. They are called **flatbed** tow trucks.

Do tow trucks come in different sizes?

Tow trucks come in several sizes. Small ones can tow cars and small trucks. Large ones can tow big trucks and buses.

This smaller tow truck is used for smaller jobs.

This tow truck will take
the damaged car
to the repair shop.

Are tow trucks useful?

Tow trucks are used all over the world. They lift and pull heavy loads. They keep our roads safer. They save lots of time and hard work. Tow trucks are very useful!

GLOSSARY

boom (BOOM) A boom is a long arm that holds something up.

cab (KAB) A machine's cab is the area where the driver sits.

engine (EN-jun) An engine is a machine that makes something move.

flatbed (FLAT-bed) Flatbed trucks or trailers have a big, flat body for carrying things.

vehicles (VEE-uh-kullz) Vehicles are things that carry people or goods.

winch (WINCH) A winch is a machine that raises or pulls things by winding a cable.

BOOKS

Pomerantz, Charlotte, and R. W. Alley (illustrator). *How Many Trucks Can a Tow Truck Tow?* New York: Random House, 1997.

Teitelbaum, Michael. *If I Could Drive a Tow Truck.* New York: Scholastic, 2003.

WEB SITES

Visit our Web site for lots of links about tow trucks: **childsworld.com/links**

Note to parents, teachers, and librarians: We routinely check our Web links to make sure they're safe, active sites—so encourage your readers to check them out!

INDEX

ABOUT THE AUTHOR

Even as a child, Cynthia Amoroso knew she wanted to be a writer. She is always working to involve kids in reading and writing, and she loves spending time in the children's section of the library or bookstore. Cynthia enjoys gardening, traveling, and having fun with friends and family.